John E. Law's

!TICKETBOOK!

:

DEDICATION

This book is dedicated to the proposition that everyone in life is entitled to be treated courteously and efficiently. You know, fair and square . . .

When that doesn't happen, write up the offender, serve them one of the tickets from this book.

There are two versions of tickets included in this book. The first set is intended to be written to jerks who take advantage. Chiselers. Folks who think rules of decorum, and the rule of law for that matter, don't apply to them. Write them up when they trespass.

The second set of tickets are intended for the idiots who park without authority in handicapped zones. Their lame, self-obsessed excuses range from,; " I'll only be a minute," "The parking lot is full," to "There's other empty handicapped spaces they can park in..."

For this class of louts we have dedicated a special ticket to be awarded.

You don't have to tear our the tickets. You have a copy machine, right?

We suggest touching up the black-and-white-only handicap offender tickets with a blue sharpie.

- The Editors

!VIOLATION!

Of Common Courtesy and/or Common Sense

(Check off each, individual infraction)

- Failure to provide common courtesy
- Outright rude behavior
- Lazy and/or sloppy performance
- Inappropriate behavior
- Failure to count change correctly
- Deceit
- Passive-aggression
- Arrogance
- Bragging
- Unfair arguing
- Bullying
- Reckless driving (includes stupid moves)
- Being Stubborn beyond belief
- Stealing a parking place
- Being meaner than a snake.
- Unauthorized parking in handicapped zone
- Incredibly bad taste
- Unscrupulous behavior
- Hateful mouth

COMMENTS:

Signature_____

!VIOLATION!

Of Common Courtesy and/or Common Sense

(Check off each, individual infraction)

- Failure to provide common courtesy
- Outright rude behavior
- Lazy and/or sloppy performance
- Inappropriate behavior
- Failure to count change correctly
- Deceit
- Passive-aggression
- Arrogance
- Bragging
- Unfair arguing
- Bullying
- Reckless driving (includes stupid moves)
- Being Stubborn beyond belief
- Stealing a parking place
- Being meaner than a snake.
- Unauthorized parking in handicapped zone
- Incredibly bad taste
- Unscrupulous behavior
- Hateful mouth

COMMENTS:

Signature_____

!VIOLATION!

Of Common Courtesy and/or Common Sense

(Check off each, individual infraction)

- Failure to provide common courtesy
- Outright rude behavior
- Lazy and/or sloppy performance
- Inappropriate behavior
- Failure to count change correctly
- Deceit
- Passive-aggression
- Arrogance
- Bragging
- Unfair arguing
- Bullying
- Reckless driving (includes stupid moves)
- Being Stubborn beyond belief
- Stealing a parking place
- Being meaner than a snake.
- Unauthorized parking in handicapped zone
- Incredibly bad taste
- Unscrupulous behavior
- Hateful mouth

COMMENTS:

Signature_____

!VIOLATION!

Of Common Courtesy and/or Common Sense

(Check off each, individual infraction)

- Failure to provide common courtesy
- Outright rude behavior
- Lazy and/or sloppy performance
- Inappropriate behavior
- Failure to count change correctly
- Deceit
- Passive-aggression
- Arrogance
- Bragging
- Unfair arguing
- Bullying
- Reckless driving (includes stupid moves)
- Being Stubborn beyond belief
- Stealing a parking place
- Being meaner than a snake.
- Unauthorized parking in handicapped zone
- Incredibly bad taste
- Unscrupulous behavior
- Hateful mouth

COMMENTS:

Signature_____

!VIOLATION!

Of Common Courtesy and/or Common Sense

(Check off each, individual infraction)

- Failure to provide common courtesy
- Outright rude behavior
- Lazy and/or sloppy performance
- Inappropriate behavior
- Failure to count change correctly
- Deceit
- Passive-aggression
- Arrogance
- Bragging
- Unfair arguing
- Bullying
- Reckless driving (includes stupid moves)
- Being Stubborn beyond belief
- Stealing a parking place
- Being meaner than a snake.
- Unauthorized parking in handicapped zone
- Incredibly bad taste
- Unscrupulous behavior
- Hateful mouth

COMMENTS:

Signature_____

!VIOLATION!

Of Common Courtesy and/or Common Sense

(Check off each, individual infraction)

- Failure to provide common courtesy
- Outright rude behavior
- Lazy and/or sloppy performance
- Inappropriate behavior
- Failure to count change correctly
- Deceit
- Passive-aggression
- Arrogance
- Bragging
- Unfair arguing
- Bullying
- Reckless driving (includes stupid moves)
- Being Stubborn beyond belief
- Stealing a parking place
- Being meaner than a snake.
- Unauthorized parking in handicapped zone
- Incredibly bad taste
- Unscrupulous behavior
- Hateful mouth

COMMENTS:

Signature_____

!VIOLATION!

Of Common Courtesy and/or Common Sense

(Check off each, individual infraction)

- Failure to provide common courtesy
- Outright rude behavior
- Lazy and/or sloppy performance
- Inappropriate behavior
- Failure to count change correctly
- Deceit
- Passive-aggression
- Arrogance
- Bragging
- Unfair arguing
- Bullying
- Reckless driving (includes stupid moves)
- Being Stubborn beyond belief
- Stealing a parking place
- Being meaner than a snake.
- Unauthorized parking in handicapped zone
- Incredibly bad taste
- Unscrupulous behavior
- Hateful mouth

COMMENTS:

Signature_____

!VIOLATION!

Of Common Courtesy and/or Common Sense

(Check off each, individual infraction)

- Failure to provide common courtesy
- Outright rude behavior
- Lazy and/or sloppy performance
- Inappropriate behavior
- Failure to count change correctly
- Deceit
- Passive-aggression
- Arrogance
- Bragging
- Unfair arguing
- Bullying
- Reckless driving (includes stupid moves)
- Being Stubborn beyond belief
- Stealing a parking place
- Being meaner than a snake.
- Unauthorized parking in handicapped zone
- Incredibly bad taste
- Unscrupulous behavior
- Hateful mouth

COMMENTS:

Signature_____

!VIOLATION!

Of Common Courtesy and/or Common Sense

(Check off each, individual infraction)

- Failure to provide common courtesy
- Outright rude behavior
- Lazy and/or sloppy performance
- Inappropriate behavior
- Failure to count change correctly
- Deceit
- Passive-aggression
- Arrogance
- Bragging
- Unfair arguing
- Bullying
- Reckless driving (includes stupid moves)
- Being Stubborn beyond belief
- Stealing a parking place
- Being meaner than a snake.
- Unauthorized parking in handicapped zone
- Incredibly bad taste
- Unscrupulous behavior
- Hateful mouth

COMMENTS:

Signature_____

!VIOLATION!

Of Common Courtesy and/or Common Sense

(Check off each, individual infraction)

- Failure to provide common courtesy
- Outright rude behavior
- Lazy and/or sloppy performance
- Inappropriate behavior
- Failure to count change correctly
- Deceit
- Passive-aggression
- Arrogance
- Bragging
- Unfair arguing
- Bullying
- Reckless driving (includes stupid moves)
- Being Stubborn beyond belief
- Stealing a parking place
- Being meaner than a snake.
- Unauthorized parking in handicapped zone
- Incredibly bad taste
- Unscrupulous behavior
- Hateful mouth

COMMENTS:

Signature_____

!VIOLATION!

Of Common Courtesy and/or Common Sense

(Check off each, individual infraction)

- Failure to provide common courtesy
- Outright rude behavior
- Lazy and/or sloppy performance
- Inappropriate behavior
- Failure to count change correctly
- Deceit
- Passive-aggression
- Arrogance
- Bragging
- Unfair arguing
- Bullying
- Reckless driving (includes stupid moves)
- Being Stubborn beyond belief
- Stealing a parking place
- Being meaner than a snake.
- Unauthorized parking in handicapped zone
- Incredibly bad taste
- Unscrupulous behavior
- Hateful mouth

COMMENTS:

Signature_____

!VIOLATION!

Of Common Courtesy and/or Common Sense

(Check off each, individual infraction)

- Failure to provide common courtesy
- Outright rude behavior
- Lazy and/or sloppy performance
- Inappropriate behavior
- Failure to count change correctly
- Deceit
- Passive-aggression
- Arrogance
- Bragging
- Unfair arguing
- Bullying
- Reckless driving (includes stupid moves)
- Being Stubborn beyond belief
- Stealing a parking place
- Being meaner than a snake.
- Unauthorized parking in handicapped zone
- Incredibly bad taste
- Unscrupulous behavior
- Hateful mouth

COMMENTS:

Signature_____

!VIOLATION!

Of Common Courtesy and/or Common Sense

(Check off each, individual infraction)

- Failure to provide common courtesy
- Outright rude behavior
- Lazy and/or sloppy performance
- Inappropriate behavior
- Failure to count change correctly
- Deceit
- Passive-aggression
- Arrogance
- Bragging
- Unfair arguing
- Bullying
- Reckless driving (includes stupid moves)
- Being Stubborn beyond belief
- Stealing a parking place
- Being meaner than a snake.
- Unauthorized parking in handicapped zone
- Incredibly bad taste
- Unscrupulous behavior
- Hateful mouth

COMMENTS:

Signature_____

!VIOLATION!

Of Common Courtesy and/or Common Sense

(Check off each, individual infraction)

- Failure to provide common courtesy
- Outright rude behavior
- Lazy and/or sloppy performance
- Inappropriate behavior
- Failure to count change correctly
- Deceit
- Passive-aggression
- Arrogance
- Bragging
- Unfair arguing
- Bullying
- Reckless driving (includes stupid moves)
- Being Stubborn beyond belief
- Stealing a parking place
- Being meaner than a snake.
- Unauthorized parking in handicapped zone
- Incredibly bad taste
- Unscrupulous behavior
- Hateful mouth

COMMENTS:

Signature_____

!VIOLATION!

Of Common Courtesy and/or Common Sense

(Check off each, individual infraction)

- Failure to provide common courtesy
- Outright rude behavior
- Lazy and/or sloppy performance
- Inappropriate behavior
- Failure to count change correctly
- Deceit
- Passive-aggression
- Arrogance
- Bragging
- Unfair arguing
- Bullying
- Reckless driving (includes stupid moves)
- Being Stubborn beyond belief
- Stealing a parking place
- Being meaner than a snake.
- Unauthorized parking in handicapped zone
- Incredibly bad taste
- Unscrupulous behavior
- Hateful mouth

COMMENTS:

Signature_____

!VIOLATION!

You are unlawfully parked in space reserved for
Handicapped Parking!

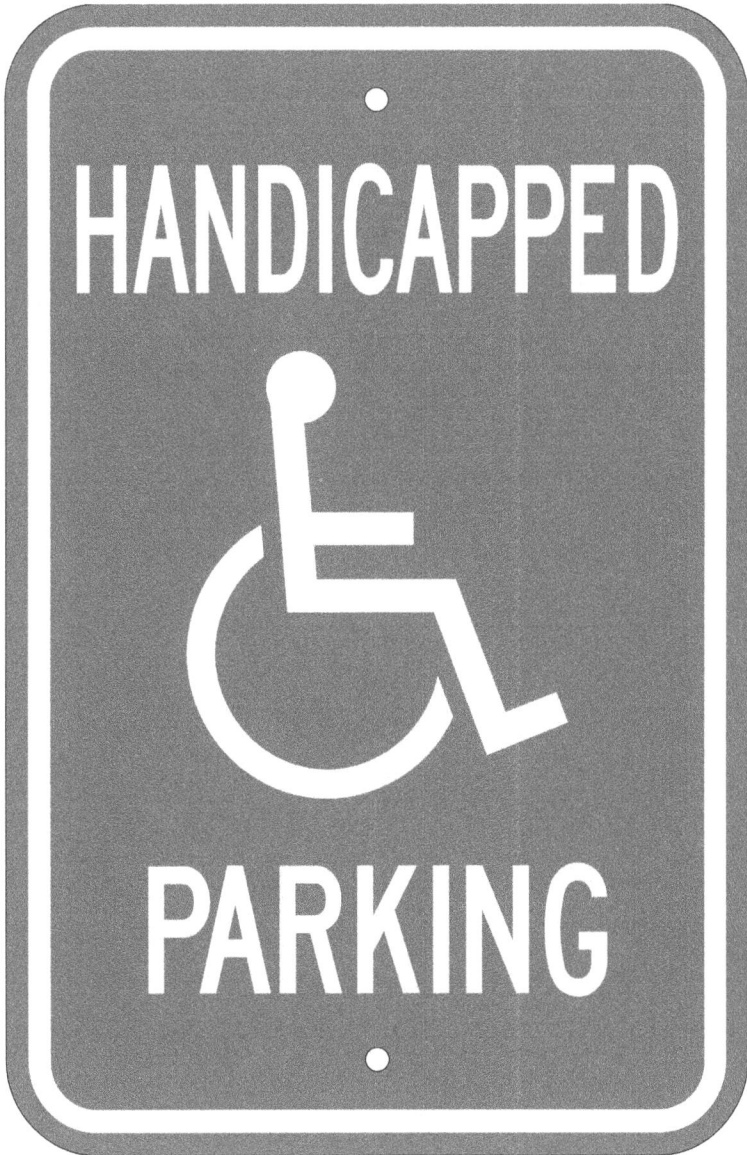

HANDICAPPED

PARKING

!VIOLATION!

You are unlawfully parked in a space reserved for
Handicapped Parking Only!

!VIOLATION!

You are unlawfully parked in a space reserved for
Handicapped Parking Only!

HANDICAPPED

PARKING

!VIOLATION!

You are unlawfully parked in a space reserved for
Handicapped Parking Only!

!VIOLATION!

You are unlawfully parked in a space reserved for
Handicapped Parking Only!

!VIOLATION!

You are unlawfully parked in a space reserved for
Handicapped Parking Only!

HANDICAPPED

PARKING

!VIOLATION!

You are unlawfully parked in a space reserved for
Handicapped Parking Only!

!VIOLATION!

You are unlawfully parked in a space reserved for
Handicapped Parking Only!

!VIOLATION!

You are unlawfully parked in a space reserved for
Handicapped Parking Only!

!VIOLATION!

You are unlawfully parked in a space reserved for
Handicapped Parking Only!

HANDICAPPED

PARKING

!VIOLATION!

You are unlawfully parked in a space reserved for
Handicapped Parking Only!

!VIOLATION!

You are unlawfully parked in a space reserved for
Handicapped Parking Only!

www.ingramcontent.com/pod-product-compliance
Lightning Source LLC
Chambersburg PA
CBHW060616030426
42337CB00018B/3081